# There Is Power In Your Pain

## Esther Kohn

There is Power In Your Pain

Copyright © 2024 Esther Kohn

ISBN 978-1-946683-60-1

Rapier Publishing Company
Dothan, Alabama 36301

www.rapierpublishing.com
Facebook: www.rapierpublishing@gmail.com
Twitter: rapierpublishing@rapierpub

Printed in the United States of America
All rights reserved under the International Copyright Law. Contents and/or cover may not be reproduced in whole or in part in any form without the consent of the Publisher or Author.

Book Cover Design: Daniel Ojedokun
Book Layout: Rapture Graphics

# DEDICATION

This book is dedicated to the Lord God, who is the head of my life. I also dedicate it to my deceased parents, Obediah and Ada Corbitt, as well as my husband, William Kohn, and my son, Jeremiah Kohn, are also deceased. To my living children, grandchildren, and to my sisters and brothers, Johnny, Venson, Wanda, and Ingrid, I say thank you. To my pastors, Jack and Annette Harmon, and to the ones who have inspired me the most, my good friend, Elder Emily Whitehurst, and my dear sister, Deborah Kohn, I express my sincerest gratitude.

This book is about "No pain, no gain." Out of your struggles, there is a life lesson to be learned. I pray when you read this book, it will make you better and not bitter.

## THANK YOU!

Esther Kohn

## TABLE OF CONTENTS

Introduction

Chapter 1: No Identity...7

Chapter 2: A Star was Reborn...9

Chapter 3: The Younger Years...14

Chapter 4: Freedom From My Past Just to Go Back to It...18

Chapter 5: The Holy Spirit Will Comfort You...20

Chapter 6: From the Pit to the Palace During Crisis... 22

Chapter 7: Spending Time with Our Aging Parents...25

Chapter 8: The Love of God is no Accident...29

Chapter 9: The Significance of the numbers Three and... 32 Thirteen

Chapter 10: When God Tells You to be Still in His...36 Presence

Chapter 11: Why Do I Say There is Power in Your...38 Pain?

Chapter 12: God Allowed Me to Go Through Some Pain...40

# There Is Power In Your Praise

## INTRODUCTION

I am not writing this book just for family and friends. I am also writing it for the people who will take the time to read it. My prayer is that the Lord will save, heal, deliver, and set people free from their bondage. Additionally, this book is written for those who are already saved, and whose goal it is to grow, mature, and go deeper in the Lord. That is, if they study the word of God, their life will be a lifetime journey of prayer, praise, and worshipping God. As you read, my prayer is that you will be a changed person; that you will confess with your mouth and believe in your heart that God has raised his Son, Jesus, from the dead, and you will, indeed, be saved.

# Esther Kohn

I'd crossed valleys, many times, tired and weak, but with the same goal, the same mind, and one heartbeat, I pressed on. Just as Jesus died on the cross, He looked at it, realizing there would be pain, but Jesus, who for the joy that was set before Him endured the cross, depising the shame, and now is sitting down at the right hand of the throne of God (Hebrews 12:2). The scripture says, "...Weeping may endureth for a night, but joy cometh in the morning," (Psalm 30:5(b).

*In pain, power always come in the morning...*

*-Esther Kohn-*

## Chapter 1 | No Identity

For years I didn't have a clue as to my identity. I was not adopted. I was the fifth child among nine siblings. But there was an empty void in my life, and I did not know how to fill it. I tried to fit in with my friends, but my dad sheltered his daughters. Both of my parents came from one parent households, and thus, were exposed to limited knowledge and information. However, what my parents lacked in academics, they made up for in character. My dad and mom were God-fearing people. They were humble and believed in taking us to the house of prayer. I didn't know much about the Holy Spirit when I was younger. The Holy Spirit was not discussed as much at that time. But I remember watching my parents pray; 'moaning and groaning in the Spirit', as it was called. They didn't have a high school degree, but they were taught by the Lord, and guided by the Holy Spirit. They made a sacrifice for their children to finish high school. I praise the Lord for our ancestors who made sacrifices.

But, I was still just going around in circles. I was at a crossroad in my life, not even knowing my purpose or destiny for being born. As a child, I knew there was something deep down inside of me that God put me here for. All I knew was that I wanted to live a clean and pure life.

I was from a small town in Alabama. My family lived in the country on a small farm. The town connected to it had two streetlights. There was a sheet factory in town, known as West Point Pepperrell, where everyone worked. Somehow, I knew there was more to life than working in a factory. Something inside of me was yearning for more. Now I know that it was God dealing with me.

I completed high school, but I wound up wanting to be like my peers and wanting to dress like them. I didn't know that was not the way. This was not what God had planned for me in my life. I'd gone to a business college to become a designer of a clothing line. This was not for me either. It was only for a season. 1st John 5:11-12 says it like this…, "And this is the record, that God hath given to us eternal life, and this life is in his Son. He that hath the Son hath life; and he that hath not the Son of God hath not life." In other words, I was still searching for my identity, but God wanted me to have the assurance that I know Him, and my identity was and is with Him!

## Chapter 2 | A Star Is Born...

Or should I say, "Esther is reborn!" The name Esther, in the Bible, means a bright and shining star. The name that I was given at birth came through the lineage of Jesus Christ our Lord and Savior. The name Esther was meant for greatness. Esther 2:17 says, "And the king loved Esther above all the women, and she obtained grace and favor in his sight more than all the virgins; so that he set the royal crown upon her head and made her queen instead of Vash'ti." Remember, there is power in your pain.

As Esther's story goes, Haman, a high ranking official of the king, had been recently promoted, and received high praises for his promotion. He received praise and reverence from everyone, that is, but Mordecai... servant of God, and Esther's uncle. Haman was extremely agitated by this, to the point of plotting Mordecai's death, and planning the execution of all the Jews... with the king's permission, of course. Knowing this, Mordecai earnestly asked his niece for help, and finished his request by asking Esther the question, "Who knoweth whether thou art come to the

# Esther Kohn

kingdom for such a time as this?" (Esther 4:14)

But this was not a simple favor. Esther understood that if she approached the king, and he didn't extend his golden scepter to her, then she would perish. Nevertheless, Queen Esther had to make a sacrifice on behalf of her people. It was life or death. Understanding this, she resolved, "If I perish, I perish." (Esther 4:16b)

Esther made preparations, had her people to go on a fast, and then began her task. Queen Esther went to the king's court and waited outside. When the king saw her, "she obtained favor in his sight; and the king held out to Esther the golden sceptre that was in his hand. (Esther 5:2) Then said the king unto her, What wilt thou, Queen Esther? And what is thy request? It shall be given thee to the half of the kingdom." (Esther 5:3) Esther invited the king and Haman to her chambers for dinner. At the second dinner, Esther announced her Jewish heritage, and told of Haman's plot to have her and the Jews of the kingdom killed. Because of Esther's faith and courage, God spared her people! She was the bright and shining star that God used to make a way for his own!

As I mentioned earlier, my name is Esther. I, too, am a bright and shining star created by the almighty God. Let me explain. Back in 2008, I remember lying in bed one morning. I did not want any distractions. I remember a king in the bible by the name of King Hezekiah. King Hezekiah was told by God, "Get your house in order, because on this day you will die." King Hezekiah turned his face to the wall, like how I did that day,

## There Is Power In Your Praise

and prayed. He reminded God of how faithful he had been in serving Him and asked for more time. This was also my prayer to God. The Lord told me, so plainly, to leave my job, at the day care facility. I asked the Lord, "Why?" My answer was, "Obey." So, I did. The more I listened and obeyed, the more He spoke. "Aha!" I thought, "The Lord still speaks!

I went to work later that day, and told them it was my last day. I thought there would have been more of a problem for the owner to hire someone else at the last minute. But, that was it. No fuss. No Muss. The owner did not ask any questions. God had worked it out in my favor.

Now it's important to mention that prior to my leaving the day care, I had my Pastor to pray for me. Specifically, I asked for prayer for my mind. I didn't know what at the time, but I knew that something was wrong with my body. For instance, I would be driving and soon find myself in a daze. I had even begun to run red lights!

One evening, I was driving and following my husband in the car ahead of me when we stopped for gas. Instead of pulling towards the gas pump, I found myself backing away from it! Oh, that was a scary situation, but somehow, my husband and I made it home. At another time, my husband and I stopped for Arabic food. The smell of the cooking oil was so strong, my head began to swim, and I left the building almost as soon as I walked in. I told my husband to take me to the Emergency Room.

There was power, even during my pain! I could have blacked

out right there, but the Holy Spirit kept me alert, so that I was able to tell the doctors in the E.R. what was happening to me. I'd retired from the City of Jacksonville, and was not able to afford insurance as a result. The doctor knew that I didn't have insurance, but for such a time as this, he performed the surgery regardless. How many of you know when God is for you, the world cannot do any harm to you! But God! He had my back and my front! What the devil meant for bad, God turned it around for my good!

My husband asked the doctor who would perform my surgery if he was saved. The doctor said yes. God gave me such a peace. Besides my parents, who were deceased, all of my family was there, waiting. The surgery was eight and a half hours long, but the Lord brought me through it.

On June 21, 2008, Dr. Prudent operated on me. They found a tumor on my brain that was about the size of a grapefruit. He told my husband that if I missed this opportunity… this time… for the doctor to remove this tumor, I might not have had another chance. Dr. Prudent was able to get 99.2% of the tumor without damaging my mobility! That is why I cannot stop praising His name! His name is Jesus, by whose stripes I was and still am healed! God was with me because I'm alive today. I came through like a bright and shining star, just like Queen Esther came through like a bright and shining star with her sacrifice, her fasting, and her praying.

There is power in sacrifice! Queen Esther sacrificed for her people. As a result, the Jews received a legal holiday known as

## There Is Power In Your Praise

Pu'rim, where they did to their enemies all that was intended for them. Likewise, Jesus made the sacrifice for us… Jews and Gentiles alike. He made the ultimate sacrifice. There is power in your pain! God the Father is in Heaven sitting on His throne. He made the creation in six days. That is God's word. He also rested on the seventh day. He's already done what He was going to do. He sent God the Son, who is Jesus. Jesus walked on this Earth for thirty-three years. At the end of thirty-three years, He gave His life for the whole world, and said, "It is Finished." Now, He is seated on the right hand side of God the Father in Heaven. God the Father sent God the Holy Spirit to Earth to dwell in us. The Holy Spirit is our comforter, advocate, and helper. God did all of this just for us because of the ultimate sacrifice of Jesus. There is power in the name of Jesus!

You cannot follow after the things of this world. Do not put your trust in man. When you do, you are not in the will of God. Rather, put all of your trust in Jesus.

The Holy Spirit wants us to listen to Him when He speaks. The Word of God says that we should be doers, as well as hearers of the Word. As we learn to listen to God, we begin to understand that He has a general will and a specific will. His general will is in the word. His specific will is asking for God's guidance and direction for your life.

Esther Kohn

## Chapter 3 | The Younger Years

Back in the day, members of my family were entrepreneurs. Therefore, it made sense to want to find out my own purpose and destiny, since my family had found theirs. My parents taught us to be around people that were successful. We weren't seen as poor. In fact, my dad had his own property. I would always tell my children to follow their heart and be the best they could be at what they were doing.

I remember I was a member of a church, teaching young people and ushering. I knew about God what I'd learned from going to church, but I didn't have a relationship with Jesus. I had to learn that the church is not in a building. It is the Holy Spirit that lives inside of us. I had been searching for Jesus for so long. In 1984, He found me. He rescued me from myself. It was on a Sunday evening. I went to the altar and was slain in the Holy Spirit. Not knowing what had happened, I realized I felt like a new person. After I left church service, I went by a 7-Eleven store and got out of the car. I began to ask the Lord what had happened to me. I heard it so plain. He said, "I just saved you." I believed that was the first time the Lord spoke to me. Aha! God still speaks! That was when the Lord began changing me. He kept drawing me closer to Him. Isaiah 55:6 says, "Seek the Lord while He may be found; Call on Him while He is near." 2 Chronicles 15:2b says, "The Lord is with you while you are with Him. If you seek Him, He will be found by you; but if you forsake Him, He will forsake you."

Now at this point, I was not around my biological family. I got married young, and I had three children. I felt as though I was going through a lot of peer pressure, even though other people around me were experiencing the same thing. I moved from a small town in Alabama to a big city in Jacksonville, Florida. My husband and I were still going to church, though he sort of strayed away. When I would ask him about going with us, he would reply, "I have forgotten more than you have learned." At that time, I felt like I needed him for my support system. In the meantime, it was in my spirit to keep searching the scriptures for answers. I remembered my Dad would always take us to Sunday School. That is what I thought a godly man does.

Again, there is power in your pain. Sometimes in life, what starts out great does not always end well. In my situation though, it did. God sees the beginning and the end. Matthew 10:30 – 32 says, "But the very hairs of your head are all numbered. Do not fear, therefore; you are of more value than many sparrows. Therefore, whoever confesses Me before men, him I will also confess before My Father who is in heaven." At this point in my life, I knew I needed to depend on the Holy Spirit, even though

# Esther Kohn

I didn't truly know who the Holy Spirit was. I was trying to be like people who I thought were godly people. I was looking at the outer appearance and not the inner man.

Confession time…I was trying to be God. But now I must repent. I'm not God! I can't create the world in six days, let alone myself in nine months. If I tried, I'd need more than a day of rest! Matthew 10:37-38 says, "He that loveth father or mother… son or daughter more than Me is not worthy of Me. And he that taketh not his cross, and followeth after Me is not worthy of Me." I was being judgmental of the saints and sinners alike. I had a zeal for God and no knowledge of God. I was just reading his Word, but I did not understand what it meant, using it out of context. But still, I'm on this journey with God. Stumbling and falling, but getting back up, and trying it again.

But God! He knew me even before I was formed in my mother's womb. Even when I didn't know what I was doing, God was watching over me, going behind me and turning my mess into a message. God is still on His throne, seated, looking, and beholding the good and the evil.

God began to speak to me at an early age. I didn't have a whole lot of friends. Our parents were particular about who we would hang around with. So, they would only let us visit our cousins. I believe that God would not connect me with people that didn't mean me any good. Now I know that God wanted to begin a good work in me, beginning with my personality. Our personality is our makeup. We cannot change that. Only God can change that. That is our being. But what we can do is listen

## There Is Power In Your Praise

to the Holy Spirit. He, the Holy Spirit, will transform our mind, which is the thinker. In other words, He changes our thought process for us to grow in grace. People! People, listen! It is so simple! He lives in us! It is like a river of living water flowing in you. Some say, "Something told me to do it that way," or "Follow the first thing that comes to your mind." Those people have been introduced to God, but they have not exercised their faith in God. It's possible that fear has tormented them, so they are afraid to step out in faith, believing they are not good enough to ask the Holy Spirit to help them. They need to have confidence in the Holy Spirit so the Holy Spirit can lead and guide them in truth and in Spirit.

Esther Kohn

## Chapter 4 | Freedom From My Past Just to Go Back to It

At this time, I came from Alabama to go to Massey Business School. The school placed me and three other students in one apartment, named St. John Apartment. Sometimes the school could not place all of the students in the dormitory, so some of the students needed to be placed in apartment buildings. One particular weekend, my friends and I were getting bored, and we decided to go for a walk along Ashley Street. Now we were from the country, and we did not know this was where ladies of the evening were.

There was a man driving alone who approached us and asked us if we wanted a ride. Mind you, we were innocent young ladies. So, we all got in the car with this young man. Overtime we got separated from each other. I supposed they were alright with the men they were with. The man I went with eventually became my husband. He gave me some alcohol, specifically a colt 45, and told me it was beer. I had never had a drink, so I drank it, trying to be sociable.

# There Is Power In Your Praise

He took me to a hotel room and raped me. He was so hurt when he found out that I was a virgin. He took me to the hospital, and afterwards, he drove me back to the apartment. There is power in your pain. I was so hurt because I wanted to save myself for my husband. But God turned our mess into a message. I did forgive my husband, but I did not tell anyone because I was embarrassed. Afterwards, I was able to share it with one of my family members. No one ever asked how my husband and I met.

The Holy Spirit said it was time to share my story. I did not tell the person who asked me. I felt in my spirit that she was too young to tell her my story. But since then, the Holy Spirit gave me this scripture. Hebrews 12:2 says, "Looking unto Jesus, the author and finisher of our faith, who for the joy that was set before Him endured the cross, despising the shame and has sat down at the right hand of the throne of God." In other words, Jesus took the guilt and shame to the cross. There is power in our pain. What we are going through is just temporary. We just made a detour that caused pain. The devil does not come with a pitchfork and a red cape. He was so beautiful, singing in the choir. But God had to kick him out of heaven. He was an imitator of God. Therefore, beware of false gods. The devil comes to kill, steal, and destroy.

Esther Kohn

## *Chapter 5* | The Holy Spirit Will Comfort You

Though there are some who are close to you who will betray you, the Holy Spirit will always teach you and keep you, if you want to be kept. Back in the day, your word was your bond. But even in the highest courts in the world, Satan is there. Luke 22:31 – 32 says, "And the Lord said, Simon, Simon! Indeed, Satan has asked for you, that he may sift you as wheat. But I have prayed for you, that your faith should not fail; and when you have returned to me, strengthen your brethren."

The Holy Spirit is our helper. If you are afraid of doing something, He will help you. Even though you are afraid, He will strengthen your heart. Psalm 27:1 says, "The Lord is my light and my salvation; whom shall I fear? The Lord is the strength of my life; of whom shall I be afraid?" Proverbs 3:7 – 8 puts it this way… "Do not be wise in your own eyes; Fear the Lord and depart from evil. It will be health to your flesh, and strength to your bones." I know the Holy Spirit will search deep down in my heart and find something that I have held inside of me. I ask the Lord to show me my pain. I need to take a deep breath. Breathe in… breathe out. Sometimes when you

## There Is Power In Your Praise

are nervous, you get butterflies in your stomach, or even sweaty palms. But remember, God has not given us the spirit of fear, but of power, love, and a sound mind. Learn to face your fears with courage, love, and kindness.

Esther Kohn

## Chapter 6 | From the Pit to the Palace During Crisis

I retired from the City of Jacksonville at 49 years old. I was always a person of few words. When I would try to express myself with words, it always came out wrong. So, I would write down what the Holy Spirit was giving me to write down. I have a brother who does the same thing. As the Holy Spirit helps me, I can be a blessing to my brother. Our gifts are not just for ourselves. We must stop apologizing for the process called sanctification. God has molded us in His image. The Holy Spirit is convicting us to go to a higher level in Him. Listen to the Holy Spirit and do not grieve Him. When the Holy Spirit comes knocking at the door of your heart, let Him in. You want Him to fix the parts of you that are broken and hurt in your life. Then you close the door instead of surrendering your life to Him. We have all done that at some point in our lives. "Lord," we say, "I'll call you later." And we do not call on Him until another crisis comes up. In His words in 2 Timothy 2:11 – 13 it says, "If we don't suffer with Him, we cannot reign

# There Is Power In Your Praise

with Him."

In 1999, there was a yearning in my spirit to do something different. I retired from my job around this time. That is when I began to feel a personal crisis as it related to young children and babies. With so many reports of babies being aborted, or even worse, being thrown in garbage cans, I began to have compassion for them. I had even seen and heard about teachers abusing children, and it broke my heart. I wanted to protect young children and babies from all the pain and agony they were going through. As a result, I started by keeping babies and young children in my residence. Soon, I took Child Development classes, eventually received my CDA license, and got a job working at the Head Start Programs.

Remembering back in my life, I had a child. I had so much pain trying to bring him into the world. The devil tried so hard to keep him from coming into this world. It started with having a dry birth. My water did not break. The doctor would not give me any pain medication until he saw the baby's head. Regardless, I named my son after my doctor. Despite all the pain I went through, my son is a sweet, caring, and compassionate young man. To add to his pain, he had asthma as a young child. God was allowing me to go through this season of caring for children. I had already acquired a love and compassion for children. There is power in our pain.

God allowed me to have a third child for seven months of his life. My friend and I carried our babies at the same time. We now have a lifelong friendship. We made a pact that when our

# Esther Kohn

babies were born, we would be Godparents to each other's baby. My baby is in heaven, but I still have a son and granddaughter. The morning I left for work, my son was smiling at me. God always picks the ripe fruit. In my busiest schedule, I didn't have a mourning period. Later, God allowed me to babysit a child from six weeks to two years old. I was able to nurture that baby, and I bonded with that baby. God gave me closure to that part of my life. God is a good God. He is a mighty good God. He turns our pain into a message.

## Chapter 7 | Spending Time with Our Aging Parents

My mom had to have an operation. The Doctor told her she had to have her gall bladder removed. At this same time, we had quite a bit happening in our own lives. My sisters had young children, and though my children were adults by then, my husband, who still worked full time, and I were in the process of planning our move back to our hometown. The enemy can raid your life only if you allow him to. For instance, my husband and I wanted to build a Jim Waltor Home, and we, therefore, decided to move back to our hometown. At the time, we didn't have a place to stay, so we lived, temporarily, with my dad. My furniture lived with him as well.

With everything and everyone living in his home, my dad eventually got tired of it all. He couldn't help but wonder when it would all be leaving. We had to have our furniture put in storage, because the house wasn't built, and wouldn't be built, we later learned, because the builders said there was not enough land. As a result, we started looking for other places to build.

# Esther Kohn

But God! Regardless of everything else, we made it home.

Mom's surgery was successful, and she lived to be 90 years old. Today, June 21st, 2022, if she were still living, she would have been 100 years old. Mom was a sweet person. She was a grateful person. I remember she would do a little happy dance while saying, "Thank you! Thank you! Thank you!!!" when given something even as small as a pair of socks. I find myself doing my happy dance whenever I sing with the praise team saying, "Thank you!!!" and I smile.

I remember mom would open her home to any and everybody and just feed them. She did not meet any strangers. Be careful. You may be entertaining angels unawares. God creates all things for His glory. When we are in tune with the Holy Spirit, He will lead and guide us in Spirit and in truth. He teaches us, tells us when to speak, and when not to speak. If we listen to the Holy Spirit, He will fight our battles.

Around this time, a large boil filled with pus had developed on my dad's neck. He had an operation to have it removed. I couldn't stand the sight of blood. But God! He gave me the strength to clean and bandage his wound. After all of the sacrifices our parents made for us, it was a blessing to be able to take care of them. It was like giving back to them.

My husband and I lived with my parents for three years. Though it was our intention to have a house built on our own property, God had other plans for us. When we moved out of my parents' home, my brother and his family moved in. What the enemy meant for bad, God turned it around, and made something good out of it. But God! He had a ram in the bush. He did us a favor. We were able to move into a house, and we didn't have to pay any rent!

We stayed there for about three months, after which time, my husband told me he was moving back to Jacksonville. God gave us favor once again. God had given my husband a vision where he was instructed to move back to Jacksonville. If my husband had not listened to God, I may not have received the type of care I received for my brain surgery! That is the reason I know this world is not our home. We are just traveling through it. God does not want us to serve idols as our God. He wants us to put all of our trust in Him rather than people, places, or things. I thank God for allowing me to put all of my trust in Him.

God has allowed me to live to tell my family's story, and it all started with snoring. Let me explain. The snoring occurred due to the opening of the nostrils being too tight, almost closed. According to my aunt, the snoring dates as far back as my granddad. I believe this was a curse from the enemy. I call it a curse because the tight opening of the nostrils, in essence, stops the oxygen from getting to the brain causing brain damage, aneurysms, and the like. The snoring was a sign of this happening. The devil never wants you to have knowledge that is good for you, but the curse has been broken over my family members!

The way we break generational curses is to repent of our ancestors' sins. We make God the head, and He turns it around. Deuteronomy 30: 19-20 says, "I call heaven and earth to record this day against you, that I have set before you life and death, blessings and curses. Therefore choose life, that both thou and thy seed may live: That thou mayest love the Lord thy God, and that thou mayest obey His voice, and that thou mayest cleave unto Him: for He is thy life, and the length of thy days: that thou mayest dwell in the land which the Lord sware unto thy fathers, Abraham, to Isaac, and to Jacob, to give them." There are consequences for not obeying the Holy Spirit when He speaks. Because of the sins of Adam and Eve, our bodies are constantly decaying. If we are obedient, we will eat the good of the land.

## Chapter 8 | The Love of God is No Accident

In 2009, Bill, my husband was in a car accident. There is power in your pain. He was driving our nephew's car. We were going to Alabama to see our parents. It was late at night, and the tires didn't have enough air in them, but we finally made it home. It was raining outside, and my husband decided he wanted to go the store. I tried to tell him not to go, but he did not listen. Here I am, getting ready for bed, when I get a call from a friend who'd seen him saying that he'd been in an accident.

By the time my brother, who'd come to get me since I didn't have a car, and I got to the scene, the rescue squad was ready to take him to a nearby hospital. I rode with my husband in the ambulance. The first hospital we were transported to was too small, so he was taken to a hospital in Birmingham, Alabama. I didn't know he was hurt so bad because he never lost consciousness. When we arrived, he had to have surgery on his right hand immediately, and afterward on his hip. But God saw him through it all. He was in the hospital for about three months.

# Esther Kohn

There is power in your pain. God was trying to get our attention. You see, when you are in the middle of a situation, you cannot see clearly. In fact, you can't see the forest for the trees. Even though I needed to take a step back and breathe, I couldn't because this situation was staring me right in the face. I was insecure and needed attention. I thought if I could get attention from my husband, it would make me feel better. But deep down inside of me was a yearning for the Holy Spirit. Man could not fill that void. Also, I was upset with my husband for being in an accident.

But God had a better plan than we had for ourselves. I believe He had to get us to the point where we had to put all of our trust in God. He wanted to make each one of us whole and complete in Christ. One cannot change each other. Only Christ can do that. Once that has been accomplished, He makes the two of us one in the Holy Spirit. Remember, marriage, like the holy trinity, involves three beings in one, with Christ being the center.

If you are a young couple who just got married, consider doing the following: study the word of God together, and learn each other's likes and dislikes. Be around couples who also love God and can share Godly wisdom with you. Do not have a proud spirit. Proverbs 16: 18-19 says, "Pride goes before destruction, and a haughty spirit before a fall. Better to be a humble spirit with the lowly, than to divide the spoil with the proud." I thank God that I am still here, and this book will help some sin sick soul. There is a song that said, "I been lied on and mistreated, but I am still here." After all the heartaches and pains, there is

## There Is Power In Your Praise

power in our pain because it makes us go deeper in the Lord. We get out of the shallow water and wade out into the deep. Then we connect with the Holy Spirit. He can use us for His glory if we get 'me, myself, and I' out of the way. If we stay focused on God, we will be perfected in the Holy Spirit.

## Chapter 9 | The Significance of the Number Three and Thirteen

The numbers three and thirteen for me and my family have been bittersweet. The Godhead is a triune, the Father, Son, and Holy Spirit. The Father, Son, and Holy Spirit were from the beginning of time. Jesus rose from the grave on the third day. Jesus, the Son of God, suffered, bled, and died on the cross for our sins. There is no other name by which we can be saved, except by the name of Jesus. The number three meant so much to me. My niece, whose life has brought me so much joy, was born on the 3rd of July. My first born, Chris, was born on January 3, 1973. His first wife passed away on January 3, 2011. He was only thirty-nine years old when this happened. His dad, my husband, had an accident on January 3, 2009, and passed away on January 3, 2021. That was a bittersweet season in our lives, but God can change bad to good. Psalm 30: 11-12 says, "Thou hast turned for me my mourning into dancing: Thou hast put off my sackcloth, and girded me with gladness; To the end that my glory may sing praise to thee, and not be silent. O Lord my God, I will give thanks unto thee forever."

# There Is Power In Your Praise

Since then, Chris has found his good thing in his wife, Angela. His dad would always call Chris his boy, I guess, because they are so much alike.

The number 13 is thought to be a bad number, but I don't see it that way. It can be viewed as the death of a matter or to the self, but the number 13 can also mean birth to the spirit: the passage on to a higher level of existence. Our apartment, a place full of good memories, was Apartment 13. I retired from the City of Jacksonville on October 13th. My brother, John, passed away at exactly the hour 3:16… John 3:16… For God so loved the world, that he gave His only begotten Son, that whosoever believeth in Him should not perish but have everlasting life.

During the early years of our marriage, I was so young and unfamiliar with faith. I would search and try to learn all I could about trusting God. I needed this faith not only for my walk with Him but also for healing. It seemed that everyone around me was trusting God for their healing. I would often wonder what would happen to me if I did not obtain the faith to do so. Will God honor my prayers and love me the same as He does them? Well, I have grown a lot. I have not perfected my faith in God, but have learned that God is faithful. He's not just to a certain group of people, but to all who love Him. God is a mystery, and His ways are past finding out. We cannot create a formula that will make God love us more than someone else; He is so much bigger than that. It Is for this reason there is faith, and it is the only real way to see Him. To every man is given a measure of faith. Even if you don't feel like you are a man or woman of faith, you are! If you will begin to exercise that faith, it will grow. Abraham, in the beginning didn't have the faith to be what God intended him to be. Through the hardships and struggles he faced, "he became" the father of faith.

Your struggles will be different from mine, and mine from yours. But just like God knew what Abraham needed to walk through to become the father of faith, He knows what each one of us need. Just listen to His voice and He will lead you. God will use circumstances of life to get you to where you need to be. He may use finances or sickness. The one thing He is working on is to increase your faith, that you, like Abraham, will become what He created you to be.

I can't help but think about Phillip's dad, as I ponder these things. He had trusted God for his healing many years and was even raised from the dead, when he was a young man. In his later years he had to have open heart surgery, his gallbladder was removed, and his kidney's had failed. The problem with his kidneys caused him to depend on dialysis for nine years. Did that take away from his walk with the Lord? Did this mean he no longer had faith? It did not! He was the sweetest Christian and trusted God to take care of him, until the day he died.

The book of Hebrews declares that some received their dead raised to life again and others died. So, were some of them greater Christians than the others? No! They were all in the faith chapter they were all equal in the kingdom.

As I said before, "God is a mystery and His ways past finding out." He knows the way that I take. And no matter where in life

## There Is Power In Your Praise

I may be, if I keep my eyes set like a flint, and serve Him with my whole heart, He will take care of me.

Esther Kohn

## Chapter 10 | When God Tells You to Be Still in His Presence

Because of technology, and being distracted by our cell phones, life itself becomes a bit hectic. We cannot or refuse to hear God. We neglect his Sabbath Day to rest in His presence. Being in His presence means going into your secret closet. Stop talking all the time and let Him speak to your spirit. Sometimes God allows us to get to the point that we are all burned out. When we are all burned out, we are too tired to resist God, and what He wants to do. The word of God says in James 4:7 that we should instead, "Submit to God, resist the devil, and he (the devil) will flee from us."

Having knowledge without wisdom and understanding is to be carnal minded. I have learned when God is speaking to you, that is between you and God. Know your purpose and what God is saying to you. The Lord does not want us to put people on pedestals. Put your trust and confidence in God, and not man.

# There Is Power In Your Praise

Love your enemies and be good to those who despitefully use you. It's easy to love someone who is lovable. Jesus wants us to go past the cross and reach out to those who are unlovable. We all have them in our family. But remember… there is power in our pain. Jesus came to the downtrodden, and those who were abused. He came for the poor in spirit. You do not have to go around the world. Minister to the people you encounter daily.

When we are spending that one-on-one time with the Lord, he starts to show you the hidden mysteries in Him. The more you study His word, the more you become alive in the Spirit. Jesus wants to know if He can trust you with His love. I think back to when I was a child growing up at home. My parents would preserve different fruits. They would go through a process. First, they would cook the fruit with sugar and spices. They'd let fruit, sugar, and spice mix get thick, and then fill their jars with the jam. Next, they would seal the jars and make sure they were airtight. Last, they would put the jars in boiling water before eventually setting them aside for our use down the road.

Just like there is a process in preserving fruits, there is a process in deeply understanding God, and allowing Him to make known those things that are hidden. The first step is Salvation. The second step is connecting with the Lord and allowing Him to mold us in His image so that we can take on His characteristics. Remember… we are a branch abiding in His vine. The third step is receiving the Holy Spirit. Some people do not get to this point. You see, when Jesus died upon the cross, He sent the Holy Spirit. The Holy Spirit, in turn, empowers us to live a Holy life.

Esther Kohn

## Chapter 11 | Why Do I Say that There is Power in Your Pain?

There is power of oneness in the unity of the Spirit. In 1 Corinthians 13:13, it says, "And now abideth faith, hope, charity, these three; but the greatest of these is charity." Let's go back to the beginning. The serpent tempted Eve. Adam and Eve ate from the tree of knowledge of good and evil. The Lord God said that Adam, as a result of eating from the tree, would have to work by the sweat of his brow, the woman would have pain when giving birth, and the serpent would have to creep on his stomach and eat the dust of the earth. Because of one man's sin, we all have a sin nature. But God had a plan.

God the Father, God the Son, and God the Holy Spirit had to have a perfect person. The virgin, Mary, had an immaculate conception. That meant Mary had to be pure, no flaws, clean without blemish. Fast forward... she had a son. His name was Jesus. There was no room in the inn when He was born in Bethlehem. There was pain when Joseph refused to marry Mary. But an angel came to him saying be not afraid. There was

# There Is Power In Your Praise

pain when baby Jesus had to be born in a stable. There was pain when Mary had to see her son whipped for every disease that came upon our bodies. There was pain when Jesus had to carry His cross. But God will not put more on us than we can bear. There were two criminals hanging beside Jesus. One said, "If you be the Son of God, save yourself and us too." The other criminal said, "This man has no sin." Jesus was mocked even until He died. But He had the power to save everyone who would receive Him in their life. He wants us to be free to serve Him, but He will not go against our will. Jesus wants us to come with all of our brokenness. He wishes that we would cast all of our cares upon Him for he cares for us.

Esther Kohn

## Chapter 12 | God Allowed Me to Go Through Some Pain

God has given us the power and authority to pray for those who are sick and lame. He gave me that gift. God gave me favor with Him. He has also given me favor with the doctors and nurses, as well as surrounded me with the love of my friends and family.

My situation was like Paul's. There was a thorn in my side. It made me draw closer to God. I had a serious operation on my brain. But God! I'm here to tell the story that God is a good and caring God. He made a way of escape for me. Jesus plus faith is everything. Mark 9:23 says, "But Jesus said unto him, if thou canst believe, all things are possible to him that believeth." The 29th verse of the same scripture says, "And he said unto them This kind can come forth by nothing but by prayer and fasting." God has got the whole world in His hand. But we must understand that everyone who says "Lord, Lord!" will not be saved. Only repent and be baptized, everyone of you, in the name of Jesus, and receive the Holy Spirit. The reason we make

# There Is Power In Your Praise

the Holy Spirit less personal is because we do not know Him.

Luke 22:69 says, "Hearafter the Son of Man will sit on the right hand of the power of God." The Holy Spirit is my helper. God knows what He is doing in our life. As you grow in grace, you may find that you lose connection with some of the people in your life. Really, I think it is because God is taking you in a different direction. The Holy Spirit wants to lead you so that God can use you. We were bought with a price. It is no longer I, but the Holy Spirit who lives on the inside of me. The prayers of the righteous availeth much!

In summary, I strongly advise young couples to spend time with their children and teach them the ways of the Lord. We are responsible for our children. They are gifts from the Lord. For this reason, make sure you know who your children's friends are. For example, teenagers should not walk or jog alone. That is why so many of our children are being abducted. Even Jesus sent his disciples into the world two by two. Please do not leave your children at home by themselves without having a trusted adult there with them. Much of the pain we go through is because we do not acknowledge God. I know very little about Human Sex Trafficking. It is here in America, the land of the free and home of the brave.

God, we repent because we have left our first love, and have gone a-whoring. Have mercy upon this Country. We have been made free by the blood of the lamb, but we are still living in bondage. You said in Your word that some things come out through fasting and praying, so we are crying out to you.

# Esther Kohn

Older women, teach the younger women. 2 Chronicles 7:14 says, "If my people, who are called by my name, will humble themselves and pray and seek my face and turn from their wicked ways, then I will hear from heaven, and I will forgive their sin and will heal their land. The people of God were thankful to Him for healing their land, physically, spiritually, and emotionally. My prayer is that we pray for the peace of Jerusalem, so that God will give us grace and mercy. Remember, without pain, there is no power.

# There Is Power In Your Praise

# Esther Kohn

About the Author:

Esther Kohn is a widower, a mother, but more importantly, a God-fearing woman of God. She was born in a small town in Alabama, where she learned to believe and trust Jesus under the nurturing foundation of her God-fearing parents. From her life's struggles, she learned to depend on God even more, realizing that struggles or setbacks are life's lessons from God, teaching her not to focus on the pain but on the One who delivers us out of them all.

She hopes this book, "There Is Power In Your Pain," will inspire everyone who reads it: teenagers, young adults, middle-aged, and the elderly. She wants you to know that there is not only power in your pain but also power in the precious Blood of the Lamb.

# There Is Power In Your Praise

www.ingramcontent.com/pod-product-compliance
Lightning Source LLC
Chambersburg PA
CBHW061806070526
44586CB00023B/2730